AROUND the Park

by Christianne C. Jones   illustrated by Ronnie Rooney

A Book About Circles

Special thanks to our advisers for their expertise:
Stuart Farm, M.Ed., Mathematics Lecturer
University of North Dakota

Susan Kesselring, M.A., Literacy Educator
Rosemount-Apple Valley-Eagan (Minnesota) School District

PICTURE WINDOW BOOKS
Minneapolis, Minnesota

Editor: Jill Kalz
Designer: Joe Anderson
Creative Director: Keith Griffin
Editorial Director: Carol Jones
The illustrations in this book were created in acrylic paints.

Picture Window Books
5115 Excelsior Boulevard
Suite 232
Minneapolis, MN 55416
877-845-8392
www.picturewindowbooks.com

Printed in the United States of America.

Library of Congress Cataloging-in-Publication Data
Jones, Christianne C.
Around the park : a book about circles / by Christianne C. Jones ; illustrated by Ronnie Rooney.
p. cm. – (Know your shapes)
Includes bibliographical references and index.
ISBN 1-4048-1572-4
1. Circles–Juvenile literature. I. Rooney, Ronnie, ill. II. Title.
QA484.J66 2006
516'.152–dc22
2005021843

Shapes are all around. You can find them everywhere you look. Shapes can be tall and skinny, short and round, long and wide. Some shapes will look the same, and some will look different, but they are all amazing. Let's find some shapes!

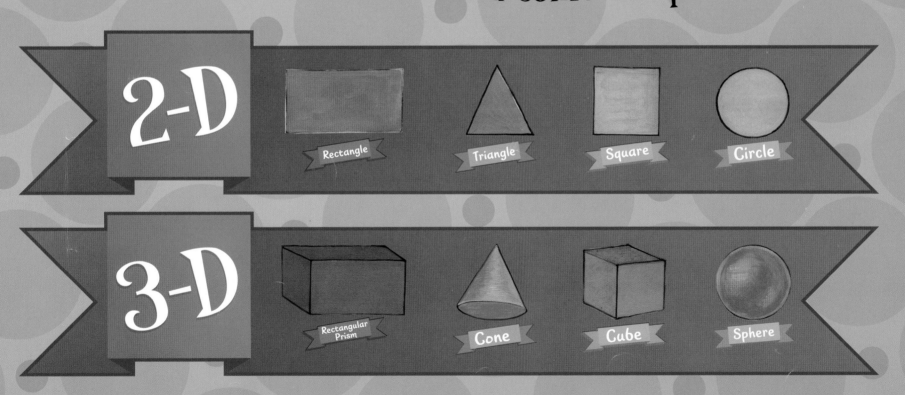

2-D
Rectangle Triangle Square Circle

3-D
Rectangular Prism Cone Cube Sphere

They have no corners and are round. Where in the park can circles be found?

4

Changing circles
make cars go and stop.

Wet circles
spray and go PLIP PLOP!

8

Spinning circles fly through the air.

Colorful circles are fun to wear.

Tasty circles
cook on the grill.

14

Shiny circles pay the bill.

16

Tiny circles decorate a face.

Speedy circles win the race.

Circles are found all around the park. But where do circles go after dark?

23

PAINT WITH CIRCLES

WHAT YOU NEED:

· A carrot, a potato, a cucumber, and a grapefruit
· A knife
· Finger paints in many colors

WHAT YOU DO:

1. Have an adult cut the carrot in half, across the middle.
2. Dip one of the carrot halves in the paint, cut side down.
3. Press the carrot on the paper plate a few times.
4. Repeat the first three steps with the potato, the cucumber, and the grapefruit. Try different colors. Fill the plate with circles, and have fun!

FUN FACTS

● Two-dimensional (2-D) shapes are flat. They have just a front and a back. Three-dimensional (3-D) shapes have a front, a back, and sides. A sphere is a 3-D circle.

● The idea for the Frisbee® started in New England. College students there played catch with empty pie tins. The tins were from the Frisbee Baking Company.

● The largest hamburger in the world weighed about as much as an elephant! It was cooked at the 2001 Burger Fest in Seymour, Wisconsin.

TO LEARN MORE

AT THE LIBRARY

Kottke, Jan. *Circles*. New York: Welcome Books, 2000.
Patilla, Peter. *Shapes*. Des Plaines, Ill.: Heinemann Library, 2000.
Schuette, Sarah L. *Circles*. Mankato, Minn.: A+ Books, 2003.
Scott, Janine. *The Shapes of Things*. Minneapolis: Compass Point Books, 200

ON THE WEB

FactHound offers a safe, fun way to find Internet sites related to this book
All of the sites on FactHound have been researched by our staff.

1. Visit *www.facthound.com*
2. Type in this special code for age-appropriate sites:
   1404815724
3. Click on the FETCH IT button.

Your trusty FactHound will fetch the best sites for you!

LOOK FOR ALL OF THE BOOKS IN THE KNOW YOUR SHAPES SERIES:

Around the Park: A Book About Circles 1-4048-1572-4
Four Sides the Same: A Book About Squares 1-4048-1574-0
Party of Three: A Book About Triangles 1-4048-1575-9
Two Short, Two Long: A Book About Rectangles 1-4048-1573-2